# God's
# high calling
## for
## women

# God's
# high calling
# for
# women

# John MacArthur

MOODY PUBLISHERS

CHICAGO

All Scripture quotations, unless otherwise indicated, are taken from the *New King James Version*. Copyright © 1982 by Thomas Nelson, Inc. Used by permission. All rights reserved.

Scripture quotations marked NASB are taken from the *New American Standard Bible*®, Copyright © 1960, 1962, 1963, 1968, 1971, 1972, 1973, 1975, 1977, 1995 by The Lockman Foundation. Used by permission. (www.Lockman.org)

Scripture quotations marked KJV are taken from the King James Version.

Interior Design:Ragont Design
Cover Design: John Hamilton Design
Cover Image: Spohn Matthieu/Getty

ISBN: 978-0-8024-5304-4

We hope you enjoy this book from Moody Publishers. Our goal is to provide high-quality, thought-provoking books and products that connect truth to your real needs and challenges. For more information on other books and products written and produced from a biblical perspective, go to www.moodypublishers. com or write to:

Moody Publishers
820 N. LaSalle Boulevard
Chicago, IL 60610

9 10 8

*Printed in the United States of America*

# Contents

# 1: God's
## high calling
## for women

### 1 Timothy 2:9

The debate over the role of women in the church has reached massive proportions. Feminist philosophy has penetrated almost every area of our society and has made significant inroads into the church. I am amazed at how many evangelical churches, colleges, and seminaries have abandoned biblical truths they previously held since their foundings. People have written books affirming new "truth" regarding the role of women in the church. Scholars have reinterpreted Scripture passages teaching the traditional roles of men and women. Some say these passages should be ignored altogether because they reflect the apostle Paul's antifemale bias. Others claim these passages were added by later editors and do not reflect the intent of the original author. The church, the foundation of the truth of God, is falling fast to the march of the feminist army.

The effort to overthrow the design of God for men and women is ultimately not a human effort. It is the effort of the archenemy of God, Satan, who uses sinful human agents to attain his goals. That's why the controversy over the role of women in the church is so tragic: the church is being deceived by the lies of Satan and is actually becoming a part of his attack. God has specific roles for men and women in society, the family, and the church that are clear in Scripture. We need to reaffirm them.

In approaching this subject, I could take a lot of time demonstrating how far-reaching feminism is. I could provide many quotes, and we could look at all kinds of incidents. We could discuss at length the schools, seminaries, and books that illustrate how pervasive the feminist movement's influence on the church has been. However, we're all aware of those influences. It seems to me most helpful to simply look at the Word of God. If we understand what the Bible says, we will be able to deal with any error we might face. There is no passage more direct and comprehensive in addressing the role of women in the church than 1 Timothy 2:9–15.

First Timothy is a letter from the apostle Paul to his son in the faith, his friend and co-laborer Timothy. Paul and Timothy had met several years before the writing of this epistle, during Paul's second missionary journey (Acts 16:1–5). When this letter was written, Paul had concluded his three missionary journeys and had just been released from his first imprisonment in Rome. After leaving prison, Paul met Timothy in Ephesus.

Timothy was pastor of the Ephesian church. Apparently word had reached Paul that things in Ephesus were not as they should be. Paul had spent three years of his ministry in Ephesus and had poured his soul into that church. In Acts 20 Paul said to the Ephesian elders that he had not failed to declare the entire Word of God to the church but had warned them night and day for three years that error would come from the outside and that evil would rise from the inside (vv. 27–31). Unfortunately, his worst fears had come to pass: the church at Ephesus had fallen into doctrinal error and ungodly patterns of living. Most significant, the leadership had been corrupted and needed to be replaced by godly leaders.

Paul met Timothy in Ephesus and personally dealt with two of the corrupt leaders, Hymenaeus and Alexander (1 Tim. 1:20). When Paul left for further ministry to the west, he left Timothy behind at Ephesus to straighten out the rest of the problems. Paul had been gone only a few weeks when he wrote this letter to Timothy to encourage him and give him direction for his ministry. First Timothy 3:14–15 gives the overall intent of the letter: "These things I write to you, though I hope to come to you shortly; but if I am delayed, I write so that you may know how you ought to conduct yourself in the house of God, which is the church of the living God, the pillar and ground of the truth." First Timothy was written to set the church in order.

One of the problem areas in the church at Ephesus was the role of women. Since the leaders of the church had fallen into doctrinal and moral error, it's not surprising that there was a negative impact on the women as well as the men. First Timothy 5:6 tells us that some women had abandoned their purity and were living only for pleasure. Some younger widows had made promises to Christ to remain single, but they were in danger of violating them because of lust, bringing condemnation upon themselves (vv. 11–12). Some had become idle, moving from house to house.

Others were becoming gossipers and busybodies (v. 13). Some had already turned aside to follow Satan (v. 15). In 2 Timothy 3:6 Paul refers to these women as gullible women loaded down with sins, led away by various lusts, making them easy prey for false teachers.

First Timothy 2 focuses on another problem involving women. Under the pretense of coming to worship God, certain women were flaunting their beauty and desecrating the worship service. Their dress and demeanor betrayed an evil intent rather than a heart of worship.

Worship is central to the church. It is not surprising that Paul discusses it early in his letter. In fact, it is the second topic he deals with in chapter 2, where he begins discussing problems in the church. The worship services at Ephesus were polluted by women who saw an opportunity to flaunt their wealth and beauty. Their sexual allure was drawing the focus away from the worship service. From his discussion of the problems women were causing in the worship services, Paul branched out into a discussion of the biblical role of women. In verse 9, we encounter the first of six essential aspects to God's high calling for women.

## THE APPEARANCE OF WOMEN (v. 9 a, c)

*"In like manner, also, that the women adorn themselves in modest apparel . . . not with braided hair or gold or pearls or costly clothing."*

The phrase "in like manner" refers back to verse 8. It introduces a new subject, but one related to the previous topic. Paul now moves to a new topic within the overall subject of how men and women should conduct themselves in worship gatherings. "In like manner" serves as a transition between different topics within a broader discussion. It is used in 1 Timothy 3:8 to make a transition from the topic of elders to that of deacons, and in verse 11 between deacons and deaconesses, all within the general subject of church leadership. Paul now moves from discussing the attitude of men in the worship service (v. 8) to that of women (vv. 9–15).

### The General Pattern

The Greek word translated "will" in verse 8 (KJV) (*boulomai*) refers to intent, purpose, determination, or command, in contrast to *thelō*, which indicates a wish. It could be translated "I command." It carries apostolic intent and divine authority. Paul is commanding men to pray and women to adorn themselves in a proper manner.

The next key word "adorn," from the Greek *kosmeō*, means "to arrange" or "to put in order." Paul is saying women should prepare themselves for worship. The Greek word translated "modest" (*kosmios*), the adjectival form of *kosmeō*, means "well-ordered" or "well-arranged."

Third, the Greek word translated "apparel" in the *New King James Version* does not refer only to clothing but can mean "demeanor" or "attitude." It encompasses a woman's total preparation for worship, involving both the attitude of the heart and proper adornment on the outside. Her clothing should reflect a heart focused on God.

The Specific Problems

Paul not only gives a general exhortation about women's appearance, but he also deals with some specific issues that were problems in Ephesus.

One specific problem was the attempt by some women *to imitate the values of their surrounding culture*. Several ancient writers have described how women dressed in the Roman culture of Paul's day, which no doubt influenced the church at Ephesus.

The writings of Juvenal, a first-century Roman

satirical poet, portray everyday life in the Roman Empire. In his sixth satire he describes women who are preoccupied with their appearance: "There is nothing that a woman will not permit herself to do, nothing that she deems shameful, and when she encircles her neck with green emeralds and fastens huge pearls to her elongated ears, so important is the business of beautification; so numerous are the tiers and stories piled one another on her head! In the meantime she pays no attention to her husband!"

First-century Roman historian Pliny the Elder told of Lollia Paulina, one-time wife of the Roman Emperor Caligula, who owned a dress worth more than a million dollars by today's standards. It was covered with emeralds and pearls, and Lollia carried receipts with her proving its value (*Natural History* 9.58).

However, in contrast to Roman society, the mystery religions of Greece had stringent rules about the appearance of women. One inscription illustrates their concern: "A consecrated woman shall not have gold ornaments, nor rouge, nor face whitening, nor a head-band, nor braided hair, nor shoes, except those made of felt or of the skins of sacrificed animals" (cited in William Barclay's *The Letters to Timothy, Titus, and Philemon*, rev. ed. [Philadelphia: Westminster, 1975], 67–68).

Both Paul and Timothy were concerned that the Ephesian church would be a godly testimony to society. For the women of the church to imitate the gaudy clothing styles of pagan women, to call attention to themselves, or to dress to entice men into illicit sexual relationships was to blaspheme the intent of the worship service.

A second specific problem was the desire by some women *to flaunt their wealth*. In the first century, poverty was widespread. The wealthy could dress in a style that was impossible for the poor to match. Today, good clothing is relatively affordable in Western society. But in New Testament times, a dress worn by a wealthy woman could cost up to 7,000 denarii (since one denarius equaled a day's wage for the average laborer, this was the equivalent of more than 19 years of an average laborer's salary). When a wealthy woman entered the worship service wearing an expensive dress, she caused a sensation that disrupted the service.

In addition to expensive clothing, rich women also displayed their wealth through elaborate hairstyles woven with expensive jewels (which is the meaning of "braided hair" in v. 9). They also wore gold rings and earrings and hung gold on their sandals and dresses.

In his work *The Sacrifices of Cain and Abel*, the

first-century Jewish philosopher Philo described a prostitute. He portrayed her as wearing many gold chains and bracelets, with her hair done up in elaborate and gaudy braids. Her eyes were marked with pencil lines, her eyebrows smothered in paint. She wore expensive clothes embroidered lavishly with flowers.

Notice that the Bible does not forbid women to braid their hair or to own gold, pearls, and fine clothes. Both the bride of Solomon (Song of Sol. 1:10) and the woman described in Proverbs 31:22 owned expensive apparel. There is an appropriate time and place for that, as affirmed by the words of Isaiah 61:10: "I will rejoice greatly in the Lord, my soul will exult in my God; for He has clothed me with garments of salvation, He has wrapped me with a robe of righteousness, as a bridegroom decks himself with a garland, and as a bride adorns herself with her jewels" (NASB).

But jewelry was (and is) often used as a way of flaunting a woman's wealth or calling attention to herself in an unwholesome way. It is that preoccupation which Paul forbids in the place of worship. When a woman dresses for the worship service to attract attention to herself, she has violated the purpose of worship (1 Peter 3:3–4).

After preaching a sermon years ago, I walked out the door of the sanctuary and was approached by a woman who was not appropriately dressed for church. She handed me an expensive piece of jewelry, a gold chain, and a note soliciting me. That is an overt example, but there are many more subtle solicitations that go on in the church. Anyone who doesn't realize this has his or her head in the sand. Look at the many pastors who fall prey to sexual sin and the many churches that have to deal with immorality and the results of pornography. That is one of the reasons for Paul's strong words in 1 Timothy 2:9–10.

John Chrysostom, a fourth-century church Father, wrote this in his homily on 1 Timothy concerning the importance of women's dressing modestly for the worship service: "What is this 'modest apparel'? Such attire as covers them completely, and decently, and not with superfluous ornaments for the one is becoming, the other is not. What? Dost thou approach God to pray with broidered hair and ornaments of gold? Art thou come to a dance? to a marriage? to a gay [humorous] procession? There such . . . costly garments, had been seasonable; here not one of them is wanted. Thou art come to pray, to supplicate for pardon of thy sins, to plead for thine offenses, beseeching the Lord, and hoping to render Him propitious to thee. . . .

Away with such hypocrisy!"

The church is a place for worship, not a show. It bothers me when I see people who claim to be Christians preoccupied with their appearance. Whenever people use the worship service to call attention to themselves, it brings great tragedy to the church.

The Proper Motives

A Christian wife should attract attention to her godly character, not to her clothing. She should show by her dress and demeanor her love and devotion to her husband. She should demonstrate a humble heart committed to worshiping God.

Likewise, single women should realize that the worship service isn't the place to try to attract men. They too should understand it is more important that someone be attracted to their godly character rather than to their outward appearance.

How can both married and single women know that they are dressed properly for the worship service? By examining their motives. A woman should ask herself, *Why am I dressed the way I am? What is my goal? Am I trying to draw attention to God or to myself? Will what I'm wearing stand out, or will it be considered appropriate for the occasion?*

First Peter 3:3-4 is a parallel passage to 1 Timothy

2:9–10. Peter writes, "Do not let your adornment be merely outward—arranging the hair, wearing gold, or putting on fine apparel—rather let it be the hidden person of the heart, with the incorruptible beauty of a gentle and quiet spirit, which is very precious in the sight of God." Like Paul, Peter emphasized that a woman is not to be preoccupied with what she wears but with who she is.

## THE ATTITUDE OF WOMEN (v. 9b)

*"With godly fear and sobriety."*

### Godly Fear

The Greek word translated "godly fear" (*aidōs*) refers to modesty mixed with humility. It connotes a sense of shame—not shame in being a woman but shame in inciting lust or distracting others from proper worship of God. A woman with a proper sense of shame will not dress to be a source of temptation. *Aidōs* implies morally rejecting anything dishonorable to God. A woman who is grieved over the possibility of offending God will not do anything to cause someone to stumble.

A godly woman hates sin so much that she would avoid anything that would engender sin in anyone.

This is certainly consistent with the words of our Lord, who said,

> Whoever causes one of these little ones who believe in Me to stumble, it would be better for him to have a heavy millstone hung around his neck, and that he be drowned in the depth of the sea. Woe to the world because of its stumbling blocks! For it is inevitable that stumbling blocks come; but woe to that man through whom the stumbling block comes! . . . See that you do not despise one of these little ones, for I say to you, that their angels in heaven continually see the face of My Father who is in heaven. (Matt. 18:6–7, 10 NASB)

## Self-Control

"Sobriety" (Gk., *sōphrosunē*) is better translated "self-control." In extra-biblical literature, *sōphrosunē* is used to speak of totally controlling one's sexual passions and desires. The Greeks valued this virtue highly. Euripides called it "the fairest gift of the gods" (Marvin R. Vincent, *Word Studies in the New Testament* [Grand Rapids: Eerdmans, 1946], 4:224). In *The Republic*, Plato says it is one of the four cardinal virtues.

There are dangers to failing to exercise self-control, both to the leaders of the church and to the congregations to which Paul writes. In 1 Timothy 3 Paul says that both elders and deacons in the church must be "the husband of one wife" (vv. 2, 12). That phrase can be literally translated as "a one-woman man." A man in a leadership role in the church must be totally devoted to his wife. I believe one of the major problems at Ephesus was that the men were not faithful to their wives. Satan attacked the church by bringing alluring women into the church to seduce the men. He continues to do so today.

Congregations are similarly affected by failing to exercise self-control. For example, in the situation of the Ephesian church in 1 Timothy 5:14, Paul stresses the importance of younger widows remarrying. Paul knew that single women with strong desires for marriage were a potential danger to the purity of the church. And that's true in our day, too.

The point of all this is obvious. The church can be a place where worship happens, or the church can be a place devoted wholeheartedly to people putting on a show. This is what so deeply bothers me when I see Christian television and find people who say they represent Christianity, people who claim to be workers and servants of the Lord, who betray an absolutely consuming preoccupation with their own appearance. It's the antithesis of everything they claim, and certainly should not mark the church. But there were some self-centered women who were using the occasion of the church meeting together to call attention to themselves, flaunt their beauty, flaunt their wealth, their attractiveness before men because they lacked humility, meekness, and modesty and control over their own desires. This brings great tragedy to the church.

In Titus 2:4–5 Paul instructs Titus regarding the congregation at Crete that older women are to teach young women "to be sober, to love their husbands, to love their children, to be discreet, chaste, keepers at home, good, obedient to their own husbands, that the Word of God be not blasphemed" (KJV). Instead of doing good, some women were causing problems in the congregation.

Another example can be found in the congregation at Corinth. In 1 Corinthians 5 Paul rebukes the Corinthians for tolerating a situation involving sexual sin. The sexual sin was a form of incest: a man having an affair with his father's wife (his stepmother). Instead of mourning over that sin, the Corinthians were boasting about it (v. 2). According to 1 Corinthians 6:13, they attempted to justify it by quoting what was perhaps a common Greek proverb: "Foods for the body and the body for foods." That is to say that sex, like eating, is merely a biological function. But Paul warned the Corinthians to flee from sexual sin (v. 18). I believe that the problem concerning women with improper motives plagued the church at Corinth as well as the churches in Ephesus and Crete.

Failure to exercise self-control has its consequences and leads to judgment. In Isaiah 3:16-26 God pronounces judgment on women who dress to draw attention to themselves:

Moreover the Lord says:

"Because the daughters of Zion are haughty,
And walk with outstretched necks
And wanton eyes,
Walking and mincing as they go,
Making a jingling with their feet,
Therefore the Lord will strike with a scab
The crown of the head of the daughters of Zion,
And the Lord will uncover their secret parts."
In that day the Lord will take away the finery:
The jingling anklets, the scarves, and the crescents;
The pendants, the bracelets, and the veils;
The headdresses, the leg ornaments, and the headbands;
The perfume boxes, the charms, and the rings;
The nose jewels, the festal apparel, and the mantles;

The outer garments, the purses, and the mirrors;
The fine linen, the turbans, and the robes.

And so it shall be:

Instead of a sweet smell there will be a stench;
Instead of a sash, a rope;
Instead of well-set hair, baldness;
Instead of a rich robe, a girding of sackcloth;
And branding instead of beauty.
Your men shall fall by the sword,
And your mighty in the war.
Her gates shall lament and mourn,
And she being desolate shall sit on the ground.

Wearing jewelry or expensive clothing is not evil, but wearing them for evil purposes is. Clothing that reflects impure motives has no place in the church.

# Review

1. Who is behind the attack on the God-designed roles for men and women?

2. Describe the circumstances that prompted Paul to write 1 Timothy.

3. What was Paul's main purpose in writing 1 Timothy (3:14-15)?

4. What were some of the problems involving the women in the Ephesian church?

5. What is the significance of the phrase "in like manner" in verse 9?

6. Describe the cultural setting in which the Ephesian church found itself regarding women's clothing.

7. True or false: According to the Bible, it is always wrong for women to wear expensive jewelry and clothes.

8. How can a woman know if she is properly dressed to attend the worship service?

9. A woman is not to be preoccupied with _____ _____ _____ but _____ _____ _____ .

10. What should be a woman's attitude toward distracting someone from worshiping God?

11. Why might Paul have included "husband of one wife" as one of the qualifications for church leaders?

12. How did the Corinthians defend their toleration of sexual sin (cf. 1 Cor. 6:18)?

13. What is Paul's counsel on how to avoid sexual sin (cf. 1 Cor. 6:18)?

# Reflect

1. First Timothy 2:9 stresses the importance of preparing for the worship service. When you go to church, the issue is not just how well prepared the preacher and the musicians are but how well you are prepared to worship God. As you prepare for the worship service, ask yourself: *Am I sincere? Is my attention focused on God? Am I coming to worship God knowing His acceptance of me is based solely on what Christ has done for me? Am I coming with a pure heart, having dealt with any sin in my life? Am I coming to be a spectator or a participant?*

2. Although 1 Timothy 2:9 teaches the importance of women's attitudes and dress in preventing sexual sin, men also have a responsibility. In 2 Timothy 2:22 Paul instructs Timothy to flee from lust. Men, when you see a provocatively dressed woman (in or out of the worship service), what is your reaction? Do you stare? Or can you say with Job, "I have made a covenant with my eyes; why then should I look upon a young woman" (Job 31:1)? Are you obeying Paul's command to flee from sexual sin, or are you courting it by reading books, looking at magazines, watching TV programs and movies, or viewing Internet sites that you know are wrong? Memorize Job 31:1, 1 Corinthians 6:18, and 2 Timothy 2:22. Then put their teaching into practice by making yourself accountable to a spiritually mature brother in Christ for your thought life and your reading and viewing habits.

# 2: God's
## high calling for women

1 Timothy 2:10–11

One of the problems facing Timothy in the Ephesian church was that some women were usurping the role of men, desiring to be the official teachers. Other women were desecrating the worship service by coming with wrong attitudes and improper dress. Their behavior contradicted their profession to know and worship God. In 1 Timothy 2:9–15 Paul gives instruction on the role of women in the church—a topic relevant to today.

The contemporary destruction of God's purpose in creating women is very tragic. The role and function of women today and consequently their divine design and their ultimate well-being in life, their meaning and sense of satisfaction, is being continually attacked and perverted. The sad thing is women are not the winners but the victims of this. Women are being told to be bold, to be assertive, to be independent, to be competitive, to take leadership, exert authority, be the breadwinner, rise to the same functional level as men, and not take a backseat to anything in that regard. Sadly, there are churches and evangelical institutions, colleges, and seminaries that have bought into this philosophy even though the Word of God is absolutely clear on the matter.

They are willing in this postmodern day, over the last generation, to reject all of the Bible's teaching, or to twist and turn it to fit new attitudes, or simply abandon centuries of Christian belief. This is tragic because women are not best-served by this; they are ill served by being cast into roles for which God never intended them to be a part.

I was thinking recently that if I could identify one single *attitude* biblically that would be the supreme attitude of all attitudes, the most desirable from God's viewpoint would be *humility*. If I were to identify one *activity* as being most desirable, it would be that of *service*.

Combining the two, I would say the Bible teaches

that the supreme endeavor for believers is *humble service*. For a woman then to offer humble service is for her to have a head start on men in being able to reach the highest level of God's intention for His creatures. Her loftiest goals are found in the humble service God has designed her for, under the direction and protection of men.  And when that is perverted, chaos results in society and chaos results in the church.

This is something we're dealing with in our society, but it is not something that only our society has faced. We go right back into 1 Timothy and we find they were having a similar problem there. Certain women in that church were living impurely or improperly. We find that in chapter five.

But not only were some women living in an ungodly and an impure way, there were women who were usurping the role of the men in the church. They were desirous of leadership. There were women who were flaunting their physical form and beauty in the worship of the church and becoming a severe distraction. They were sensually trying to lure men away from their own wives, and there were some very serious matters the church needed to deal with in this regard.

In 1 Timothy 2:9–15, Paul deals with these two issues: the issue of women leading in the church and the issue of women appearing indecently in the church. They were coming to worship God when in fact their desire was to present themselves in some indecent fashion for a self-serving, lustful end. Paul then instructed Timothy to give appropriate teaching to the church concerning such indecency of conduct and such perversion of role.

As we look at verses 9 to 15, there are six elements that outline the woman's design and speak to a woman's place in the church. Paul refers to their appearance, their attitude, their testimony, their role, their design, and their contribution.

In our previous chapter, we discussed the appearance of women and the attitude of women in 1 Timothy 2:9. In this chapter, we'll take a look at the testimony of women and the role of women.

## THE TESTIMONY OF WOMEN (v. 10)

*"But, which is proper for women professing godliness, with good works."*

### The Importance of a Woman's Testimony

Paul was concerned that a woman's testimony be consistent. "Proper" (*agathōn*) refers to works that are genuinely good, not merely good in appearance. The

Greek word translated "professing" (*epangellō*) means "to make a public announcement." Any woman who has made a public announcement about her commitment to the Lord should conduct herself in a manner consistent with such a profession.

"Godliness" (Gk., *theosebeia*) has the basic meaning of reverence to God. When a person claims to be a Christian, he or she is claiming to worship and serve God. Any woman who claims to serve and worship God should conduct herself in godliness. To do otherwise would bring reproach on the name of Christ. A woman cannot claim to fear God and yet disregard what His Word says about her behavior. She cannot contradict God's design for her in the church and yet claim to love Him.

## The Desecration of a Woman's Testimony

Verse 10 points out a major problem with the contemporary feminist movement in the church. A woman who wants to serve and honor God cannot show disregard for what He says in His Word about the role of women.

## The Substance of a Woman's Testimony

The testimony of a woman professing godliness is a life of good works. Righteous deeds demonstrate the genuineness of her faith. The same is true for men.

The concept of a woman's testimony is critical. However, in this passage, Paul mentions it only briefly. He then continues in verses 11–12 with a discussion of his next concern, one with enormous ramifications that extends throughout this chapter of our discussion and into the next.

## THE ROLE OF WOMEN (vv. 11–12)

*"Let a woman learn in silence with all submission. And I do not permit a woman to teach or to have authority over a man, but to be in silence."*

Paul continues his discussion of women's duties by defining their role as learners rather than teachers during the public worship. Although they are not to be the public teachers in that context, neither are women to be shut out of the learning process, as generally happened in ancient times.

The Greek word translated "learn" (*manthanō*) is in the imperative mood, indicating it is a command. Paul commanded that women be taught. Since this section of 1 Timothy is discussing how the church is to conduct itself (see 3:15), the learning is to take place when the church meets. We see from Acts 2:42 that learning was a high priority when the early church met. Paul *commanded* that women be a part of the learning process.

Despite the claims of some to the contrary, teaching and worship are not mutually exclusive. Rather, knowledge of God and His Word helps to stimulate worship. Worship is to be in spirit *and* in truth (John 4:20–24).

One of the problems in the Ephesian church was that some Jewish believers were still holding on to their Judaism. They were preoccupied with genealogies (1 Tim. 1:4). Some desired to be recognized as teachers of the law (1 Tim. 1:7). Jewish tradition of that day had a low view of women. They were not usually given opportunities to learn. They were not forbidden to come to the synagogue, but they were not encouraged to come, either. Most rabbis refused to greet women in public and believed that teaching them was a waste of time. Thus, although women were not completely forbidden to learn, they were not encouraged to do so either.

The Jewish view of teaching women no doubt led to a certain amount of suppression of them in the church at Ephesus. In reaction to that extreme position, some of the women were determined to rise to leadership. First Timothy 2:12 says women were teaching and exercising authority over men. Paul told them to stop. But before Paul dealt with the problem of women usurping the role of men, he first settled the question of whether women have a right to learn. His brief statement "let a woman learn" shows there's equality of the sexes in spiritual life and blessing.

## The Role of Women in the Old Testament

In spite of Jewish tradition, the Old Testament *does not* teach that women are inferior. The Old Testament teaches that women are spiritually equal to men. They had the same responsibilities as men, which included the command to obey the law. In Exodus 20 the Ten Commandments are given to both men and women. From the beginning, God laid down the principle that both sexes are responsible for obeying His laws.

Deuteronomy 6:6–7 says that both men and women are responsible to teach their children to obey God's law and to love Him. Proverbs 6:20 says, "My son, keep your father's command, and do not forsake the law of your mother." The assumption is that both sexes are responsible to teach the law of God to their children, which means they must know that law.

Both men and women in the Old Testament are commanded to participate in the festivals. In Exodus

12 both are involved in the Passover, one of the greatest celebrations of the Jewish calendar.

Both men and women were granted the same protection concerning crimes. Penalties given for crimes against women are the same as those for crimes against men (cf. Ex. 21:28–32). God values equally the life of a man and the life of a woman.

Women also took the same vows as men. The greatest vow an Israelite could take was the Nazirite vow. It was a vow of separation from the world and devotion to God. Women as well as men could take this vow (Num. 6:2).

Both men and women had the same access to God. God dealt directly with women in the Old Testament; He didn't go through men every time He wanted to communicate with them. For example, the angel of the Lord (a pre-incarnate manifestation of Christ) appeared to Hagar (Gen. 16:8–13) and the mother of Samson (Judg. 13:2–5).

Women also held the same privileges as men in the Old Testament. Women as well as men served God in special ways. Nehemiah 7:67 tells of a choir made up of 245 singing men and women. They led the people to praise God through music. According to Exodus 38:8, women served at the door of the Tabernacle, possibly to instruct women who were coming to worship or to clean the Tabernacle grounds. From such passages as Deuteronomy 12:10–12, 1 Samuel 1, and 2 Samuel 6, we learn that women shared in the great national celebrations of Israel.

Thus, women had the same responsibility to obey the law and teach it to their children as did men. They participated in the religious life of Israel and served God. Far from giving women a secondary status, the Old Testament granted them spiritual equality with men.

Yet although women shared *spiritual equality* with men in the Old Testament, they did not have the same *role*. (Nonetheless, that does not diminish their spirituality.)

Women in Old Testament times did not serve as leaders. There were no women rulers in the history of either Israel or Judah. Deborah was a judge who acted primarily in the role of an arbiter, not as an ongoing leader. That explains why she called on Barak when needing military leadership against the Canaanites (Judg. 4–5). Queen Athaliah was a usurper and not a legitimate ruler (2 Kings 11). There is no mention of women priests in the Old Testament. As far as we know, no woman wrote any portion of the Old Testament.

In addition, women had no ongoing prophetic ministry. No woman in the Old Testament had an ongoing prophetic ministry such as that of Elisha or Elijah. There are five women in the Old Testament who are referred to as prophetesses.

*1. Miriam:* Miriam was the sister of Moses and is called a prophetess in Exodus 15:20. Perhaps she is called a prophetess because she gives a brief revelation in verse 21. We know of no other occasion when she acted in the prophetic office.

*2. Deborah:* Deborah is described as a prophetess in Judges 4:4 because God used her to give a direct revelation to Barak. We know of no other occasion when she engaged in ongoing prophetic work.

*3. Huldah:* Huldah gave revelation from God to Hilkiah the priest and other men about the coming judgment on Jerusalem and Judah (2 Kings 22:14–22; 2 Chron. 34:22–28). There is no other recorded instance of her speaking as a prophetess.

*4. Noadiah:* Noadiah was a false prophetess who opposed the work of Nehemiah in rebuilding the walls of Jerusalem (Neh. 6:14).

*5. The wife of Isaiah:* Isaiah's wife is called a prophetess in Isaiah 8:3 because she gives birth to a child whose name had prophetic meaning. There is no record of her speaking a prophecy. This passage indicates that the word *prophetess* can be used in a general way.

The Old Testament differentiates the *role* of women from men. Women are not inferior to men but have a different role.

## The Role of Women in the New Testament

The New Testament also teaches the same spiritual equality of men and women, yet provides distinctive roles for each. Galatians 3:28 declares the spiritual equality of men and women: "There is neither Jew nor Greek, there is neither slave nor free, there is neither male nor female; for you are all one in Christ Jesus." In the context of Galatians 3, the oneness spoken of here is the oneness of salvation. That is clear from verses 13–27. Paul's point is that all people—Jews and Gentiles, slaves and free men, men and women—have equal access to the salvation that is in Christ. The passage has nothing to do with the role of women in the church, nor does it teach that all differences are eliminated among Christians. A Jewish person did not cease to be Jewish when he or she became a Christian, and slaves did not automatically become free people. Some distinctions were retained.

While many use that verse to justify women assuming leadership roles in the church, the context shows that Paul is speaking of salvation (Gal. 3:22, 24, 26, 27). Robert Saucy writes,

The interpretive question [in Gal. 3:28] is: What is the distinction between male and female which is overcome in Christ? To phrase it another way in light of the apostle's statement "for you are all one in Christ Jesus," what is the "oneness" which male and female share in Christ? We would like to suggest . . . that the answers to these questions do not concern the functional order between man and woman at all. Rather the issue, as in the other two pairs mentioned [Jews and Greeks, slaves and freemen], concerns spiritual status before God. . . . To impart the issue of the functional orders of human society into this passage is to impute a meaning not justified by a valid contextual exegesis. There is therefore no more basis for abolishing the order between man and woman in the church from Galatians 3:28 than for abolishing an order between believing parents and children or believing citizens and rulers. For they are all one in Christ in or out of the organization of the church. ("The Negative Case Against the Ordination of Women," in Kenneth S. Kantzer and Stanley N. Gundry, eds., *Perspectives on Evangelical Theology* (Grand Rapids: Baker, 1979, 281–82)

Men and women also share the same spiritual responsibilities. All the commands, promises, and blessings of the New Testament are given equally to men and women. We all have the same spiritual resources and the same spiritual responsibilities.

It is interesting that Jesus first revealed He was the Messiah to a woman (John 4). Jesus healed women (Matt. 8:14–15), showing them as much compassion as He did men. He taught women (Luke 10:38–42) and allowed them to minister to Him (Luke 8:3). At the cross, the women remained after the men had fled (Matt. 27:55–56). A woman first saw the resurrected Christ (Mark 16:9; John 20:11–18).

However, as in the Old Testament, men and women shared separate roles in the New Testament. Women did not serve as leaders. There is no record in the New Testament of a woman apostle, pastor, teacher, evangelist, or elder. The New Testament does not record any sermon or teaching by a woman.

Second, women did not have an ongoing prophetic role. Some argue that the daughters of Philip prophesied (Acts 21:9). However, they are not referred to as prophetesses, nor is there any indication of how often they prophesied. They may have spoken on only one occasion, as Deborah and Miriam apparently did in the Old Testament. The New Testament records other occasions when women spoke the word of God. Mary, the mother of Jesus, speaks the word of God in Luke 1:46-55. First Corinthians 11:5 says that women who prophesy are to have their heads covered. Acts 2:17 speaks of women prophesying. The Greek word translated "prophesy" simply means "to speak forth" or "to proclaim." There are times and places when women speak the word of God, but that is distinctly different from being identified as a pastor, teacher, elder, evangelist, or apostle.

Women have an important place in the plan of God, and they are equal with men spiritually. However, they are not to function in the same role as men. Because women are spiritually equal, Paul insisted that they be given the same opportunities to learn as men. Women cannot teach spiritual truths to their children (as Timothy's mother and grandmother did), lead people to Christ, or obey God if they are not given the opportunity to learn. Paul wanted to clearly teach that the differences in roles between men and women do not in any way imply the spiritual inferiority of women. He said, "Let a woman *learn*" (v. 11, emphasis added).

I want to share something very personal. I've thanked God over the forty years at my church for the tremendous ministry women have had. I want you to know Grace Community Church wouldn't be in the place it's in now—being so blessed by God—if it were not for the women of the church. I have never seen a church with more spiritually proactive, faithful, Christ-exalting women. I have never seen a church where women feel more freedom, more liberty, more joy, and more exhilaration in doing that ministry.

Yet from the outside, my church is sometimes accused of being chauvinistic, narrow-minded, antiquated, and traditional. We're accused of belonging to the dinosaur age. But actually I praise God that for all the years of my ministry there, a high priority has been to let women learn. I rejoice that women were learning at Grace Church from the very earliest days when on Tuesday mornings I taught a women's Bible study, right on to today where we now have women learning in multiple times, locations, capacities, and even languages. We have our women's Bible study, Every Woman's Grace, in Spanish, Korean, and Filipino (as well, of course, in English.) Women of all backgrounds are learning God's Word.

It strengthens every dimension of the life of the church. God can bless many of my church's men, and they can be grateful to Him that their wives have grown and learned things from the Word of God that can enrich their own lives and families.

I praise God for that. I don't believe, as the media and people outside often try to paint it, that we have a whole lot of deprived women who are bound in a traditionalism that's not true to contemporary culture. I believe that our women at Grace Community Church have experienced the true freedom to be all that God wants them to be within the role God has designed for them. I thank God for the commitment of the women of my church and the entire church to the necessity that women have to learn. So Paul says, "Let the women learn."

# Review

1. What were some of the problems relating to women in the Ephesian church?

2. Why is it important that a woman's testimony match her profession of faith?

3. The testimony of a woman professing godliness is a life of _____ _____ .

4. According to Acts 2:42, _____was a high priority when the early church gathered together.

5. In your own words, summarize the place of women in first-century Judaism.

6. True or false: The contemporary Jewish view of women influenced the way women were being treated in the Ephesian church.

7. True or false: The Old Testament, in agreement with Jewish tradition, teaches that women are inferior spiritually.

8. Name some of the spiritual responsibilities women shared with men in the Old Testament.

9. How did the role of women in the Old Testament differ from that of men?

10. Does Galatians 3:28 teach that all differences

between men and women have been eliminated? Explain.

11. Did Jesus treat women as inferior to men? Support your answer from Scripture.

12. Why is it important for women to learn spiritual truth?

# Reflect

1. The church at Ephesus was influenced by the
prevailing views of society regarding women.
The same could be said about the church today.
The church is often influenced by the world instead of being an influence on the world. Are
your views shaped by the opinions of society or
by God's Word? Think about your position on
such issues as women's roles, abortion, homo-
sexuality, creation and evolution, the Christian's
responsibility to government, lawsuits, and di-
vorce and remarriage. Spend time in prayer and
ask God to give you the courage to take a stand
on these issues based on His Word—no matter
what views society propagates. Then pray that
the church as a whole will also stand firm for
God's truth.

2. Jesus ministered to all types of people, even those His culture considered inferior. He ministered to the poor, lepers, and tax collectors. Are you selective about whom you allow yourself to serve? Do you reach out to the difficult people and strangers at your church and Bible study group, or do you play it safe and stick with your friends? The next time you see a person in need and are tempted to turn away because he isn't part of your crowd, remember the example of Jesus as well as the teaching in James 2:1–9.

# 3: God's high calling for women

## 1 Timothy 2:11

Catharine Beecher was the oldest child in her family. One of her younger sisters was novelist Harriet Beecher Stowe, author of *Uncle Tom's Cabin*. Catharine grew up with a great love for children, finding joy in rearing and caring for them. Her mother was a skilled homemaker and taught her how to take care of the home.

When Catharine was sixteen her mother died, and an aunt moved in. Her aunt was noted for her neatness and ability to manage the home orderly and economically. Catharine's father eventually remarried, and her stepmother was also an expert homemaker.

Catharine, under the tutelage of those exemplary women, decided in turn to train other women for their domestic responsibilities. At the age of twenty-three she founded The Hartford Female Seminary, which trained women to be lovers of their husbands and children and keepers of the home.

In 1869 Catharine and Harriet wrote a book entitled *The American Woman's Home* (New York: J. B. Ford). They wrote,

> Woman's profession embraces the care and nursing of the body in the critical periods of infancy and sickness, the training of the human mind in the most impressionable period of childhood...and most of the government and economies of the family state. These duties of woman are as sacred and important as any ordained to man; and yet no such advantages for preparation have been accorded her, nor is there any qualified body to certify the public that a woman is duly prepared to give proper instruction in her profession. (14)

It was their desire to train women "not only to perform in the most approved manner all the manual employments of domestic life, but to honor and enjoy these duties" (14–15).

If a woman today were to establish a female seminary to train women in domestic responsibilities, she would become the laughingstock of the Western world. Training women to keep the home opposes what society teaches is important.

We are in a day when role reversal is a high priority for Satan. It would be one thing if he directed that strategy only at the world, but it is even more tragic when it infiltrates the church. The church today has definitely lost its sense of perspective and balance regarding the woman's role. I'm amazed as time passes to see an increasing number of Bible-believing people, under the pressure of the society around them, begin to change their view of the woman's role. The sad part is that they are then instructing women to deny a God-ordained pattern for a life that would bring them the highest joy.

It was a problem in the day of Catharine Beecher, it's a problem today, and it was a problem in the day when Paul wrote his first letter to Timothy. In 1 Timothy 2:9–15, the apostle provides a comprehensive treatment of the role of women in the church. In verse 9, we discussed the appearance of women and the attitude of women. In our previous chapter, we examined the testimony of women and began our discussion on the role of women, including the spiritual equality of men and women despite differing roles. In this chapter, we'll continue our study into verse 11 as we seek to understand what God's Word teaches on this vital issue of God's high calling for women.

## THE ROLE OF WOMEN (vv. 11–12)

*"Let a woman learn in silence with all submission. And I do not permit a woman to teach or to have authority over a man, but to be in silence."*

The church at Ephesus existed in a city dominated by Greek culture and religion. According to William Barclay,

> The place of women in Greek religion was low. The Temple of Aphrodite in Corinth had a thousand priestesses who were sacred prostitutes and every evening plied their trade on the city streets. The Temple of Diana in Ephesus had its hundreds of priestesses called the *Melissae* which means the bees, whose function was the same. The respectable Greek woman led a very confined life. She lived in her own quarters into which no one but her husband came. She did not even appear at meals. She never at any time appeared on the street alone; she never went to any public assembly. The fact

is that if in a Greek town Christian women had taken an active and a speaking part in its work, the Church would inevitably have gained the reputation of being the resort of loose women. (*The Letters to Timothy, Titus, and Philemon*, rev. ed. [Philadelphia: Westminster, 1975], 67)

Paul makes two points in verse 11 about women in the church: they are to learn in silence, and they are to learn in submission. The Greek word translated "silence" (*hēsuchia*) means simply silence. We'll have to determine its exact meaning from the context. The Greek word translated "subjection" is from *hupotassō*, which means "to line up under." Women are not to be rebels; they are to serve in their proper roles.

The instruction for women's silence has been misinterpreted in two ways. Those who believe women are free to preach in the church interpret "silence" as a reference to a meek and quiet spirit. They claim that this passage says women preachers or teachers are to have meek and quiet demeanors. Others turn to the opposite extreme and insist that no woman should ever speak in church under any circumstance—not even to the person she is sitting next to. However, Paul in verse 12 says women are to be silent by not teaching or exercising authority over men in the church.

### They Are to Learn in Silence
### (v. 11a; see 1 Cor. 14:34)

*"Let a woman learn in silence."*

First Corinthians 14:34 echoes the thought of 1 Timothy 2:11. Paul writes, "Let your women keep silent in the churches, for they are not permitted to speak; but they are to be submissive, as the law also says."

"Let" (*epitrepō*) is always used in the New Testament to speak of permitting someone to do what they desire to do. Paul's choice of words may imply that some women in Ephesus desired to be the public preachers, and thus have authority over the congregation—as in today's church. Paul, however, speaking as the official apostle of Jesus Christ, does not allow that. The role of the elder as evangelist or pastor-teacher is for men only.

The reason women are not to preach in the church has nothing to do with their psychological makeup or intellectual capabilities. Those who insist that subordination and equality are mutually exclusive would do well to consider Christ's relationship to the Father. While on earth, Jesus assumed a subordinate role, yet He was in no way inferior. First Corinthians 11:3

states, "But I want you to understand that Christ is the head of every man, and the man is the head of a woman, and God is the head of Christ" (NASB).

The last phrase in 1 Corinthians 14:34 says women are not to teach in the church because God's law forbids it (see Gen. 3:16).

The context of 1 Corinthians 14 indicates that the silence Paul commands is not intended to preclude women from speaking at all, but to keep them from speaking in tongues and prophesying in the church. The cultural context of this region helps shed light on this teaching.

The city of Delphi, located across the Gulf of Corinth, was the seat of a religion headed by a woman known as the Pythia, or the oracle of Delphi. To qualify for the office of priestess in this religion, a woman had to be a young virgin. Later, married women over fifty were preferred, but they were required to dress like maidens. Each priestess was a medium in contact with demonic spirits.

A man desiring to consult the oracle (no women were allowed to consult) sacrificed an animal while a few attendant priestesses evaluated the omens. If they were favorable, the man was permitted to enter the inner shrine. After entering he wrote his request on a tablet (archaeologists have excavated the shrine area and have found some of those tablets still intact), which would probably then be read to the Pythia. The Pythia sat on a tripod, allegedly over a chasm from which a mystic vapor from the ground arose. Before taking her seat, she drank water from the prophetic stream called Kassotis and ate sacred laurel leaves. In response to the question on the tablet, she uttered incoherent sounds that were interpreted (often in perfect hexameter verse) by a male prophet who stood nearby. The interpretation, which was often obscure and variable, usually left the inquirer more mystified than when he came.

That pagan practice had a negative impact on the church at Corinth. Some people came into the Corinthian assembly and uttered similar ecstatic speech, supposedly in the power of the Holy Spirit. That led to chaos in the Corinthian church. The true gifts of speaking in tongues and prophesying became confused with satanic counterfeits.

At Corinth, as in Ephesus, women flaunted their sexuality. Perhaps influenced by the Delphic religion, they sought prominent positions in the Corinthian church by abusing the gifts of speaking in tongues and prophesying.

In response to that problem, Paul wrote, "How is it, then, brethren? Whenever you come together, each of you has a psalm, has a teaching, has a tongue, has a revelation, has an interpretation. Let all things be done for edification" (1 Cor. 14:26). Paul goes on to say that no more than two or three were to speak in tongues and never without an interpreter present. Only two or three prophets were to speak, and others were to evaluate them to see if they spoke the truth (vv. 27–29). Paul's point is that God is not the author of confusion (v. 33). Finally, he instructs the women to keep silent (v. 34). They were not to speak in tongues or prophesy in the public assembly of the church.

First Timothy 2:11–12 and 1 Corinthians 14:34–35 tell us that when the church comes together, women are not to speak in tongues, prophesy, or teach the Word of God. When the church comes together the appointed men are to do the teaching.

However, that does not mean women can never speak God's truth. God used women such as Miriam (Ex. 15:20–21), Deborah (Judg. 4:4), Huldah (2 Kings 22:14–22), and Anna (Luke 2:36–38) to speak for Him. Paul spoke with various churches and synagogues during his missionary journeys, answering questions from women as well as men (cf. Acts 17:2–4). I believe there is a time and place for women to publicly offer praise to the Lord. I don't believe Paul is saying women can never serve in this capacity. But he prohibited women from taking leadership roles in the church.

## They Are to Learn in Subjection
### (v. 11b; 1 Cor. 11:3)

*"Let your women learn . . .
but they are to be submissive."*

In 1 Corinthians 11:3 Paul says, "The head of every man is Christ, and the head of woman is the man; and the head of Christ is God" (KJV). That verse teaches that women are to submit to men regarding the role of church leadership, which belongs exclusively to qualified men.

No believer argues that Christ is not the head of the man. And believers understand that God the Father is the head of Christ. Philippians 2:5–8 teaches that Christ took upon Himself the form of a servant during His incarnation. Since Christ is the head of the man and God the Father is the head of Christ, why do we debate about whether the man is the head of the woman?

In Corinth it was customary for married women to cover their heads to display their modesty. It was a sign that they were committed to their husbands and not available to other men. Men, on the other hand, had their heads uncovered as a mark of their masculinity. In the Corinthian church those cultural signs were becoming inverted: women were praying and prophesying with their heads uncovered—thus identifying themselves with the liberated women in Corinth—and the men—perhaps because of Jewish influence—were covering their heads while praying. Paul rebukes the men in verse 4: "Every man praying or prophesying, having his head covered, dishonors his head." Does that mean it is a sin for men to have something on their heads when they pray? No, not unless your culture perceives that as something feminine. In verse 5 Paul rebukes the women: "Every woman who prays or prophesies with her head uncovered dishonors her head, for that is one and the same as if her head were shaved" (a shaved head was a symbol of shame).

We should identify with our society's symbols of masculinity and femininity unless they violate Scripture or God's design for morality. Such symbols in our society can be readily discerned. We can tell the difference between a woman who looks like a woman and a woman who looks like she is rebelling against womanhood. We can look at a man and tell by the way he dresses and carries himself if he is denying the cultural symbols of masculinity.

But what about 1 Corinthians 11:5? Does this verse allow for female preachers? Some people teach that the praying and prophesying of the women in 1 Corinthians 11:5 took place during the worship service. However, the text doesn't say that. Perhaps Paul was speaking of prayer and prophecy in general. It's not until 11:18 that Paul first speaks of the formal gathering of the church: "For first of all, when you come together as a church, I hear that there are divisions among you." Prior to verse 18 he apparently was not speaking of the worship service.

Perhaps Paul is speaking in verse 5 of women praying and proclaiming the Word of God in a home Bible study or family prayer time. His point is that whenever Christians gather together, women are to maintain the decorum of submission, and men are to maintain the role of headship. If a woman was veiled when she prayed or spoke the Word of God, she attested to her womanhood and affirmed her submission to her husband. She was acknowledging that man is the image and glory of God and that she is the glory of man (v. 7). Man is symbolic of the glorious dominion of God, and woman is symbolic of the one who follows.

God designed human life to revolve around relationships. And within those relationships are differing roles. However, in our society we emphasize the individual over the relationship. Individuals focus on their rights, and they seek to satisfy themselves. In such a society there is a tendency to view everyone as having an equal role. But when women refuse to accept their God-ordained roles in the church and family, they undermine the foundational design of God for those institutions, and the stability of society is at stake.

## SOME PRACTICAL CONSIDERATIONS

### 1. When can women proclaim the Word of God?

Women can proclaim the Word of God at any time and at any place, except when the church comes together for the worship service. The New Testament gives examples of Mary and Anna speaking the truth (Luke 1:46–55; 2:36–38).

### 2. In Bible studies, can women share what they've learned?

Yes, in the right environment there is nothing wrong with a woman sharing what the Spirit of God has taught her out of the Word.

### 3. *Can women pray in public?*

Yes, women can pray in public. Acts 1:13–14 describes a prayer meeting where the disciples of Jesus as well as several women were present. There is a time and a place when it is perfectly appropriate for a woman to pray in public.

When Paul writes in 1 Timothy 2:11, "Let a woman learn in silence," he means that women are not to teach during the official meeting of the church. The responsibility of being the preacher, the teacher, or the one who leads in prayer in the worship service is a role ordained for men.

Women must stop believing the devil's lie that the only role of significance is that of leadership. People usually desire places of prominence—not to humbly serve others, but to boost their own egos and gain power and control. Leaders, however, bear a heavy burden and responsibility, and the subordinate role often is one of greater peace and happiness. Subordination is not punishment, but privilege.

# Review

1. The city of Ephesus was dominated by

   _____

   culture and religion.

2. True or false: Women enjoyed a great amount of personal freedom in Greek society, often taking an active role in the public assemblies.

3. What two points does Paul make in 1 Timothy 2:11 about the role of women in the church?

4. True or false: Paul's command that women keep silent in the church means that a woman is not to speak under any circumstances.

5. What is the reason women are not permitted to teach in the church?

6. Describe the influence the Delphic religion had on the Corinthian church.

7. How did Paul instruct the Corinthians to correct the problems in their church?

8. Why was it wrong for the Corinthian men to pray with their heads covered?

9. Does 1 Corinthians 11:5 teach that women can proclaim God's Word in the church service? Support your answer.

10. Why is it such a serious matter for women to reject the roles God has designed for them in the family and the church?

# Reflect

1. Some women in the Ephesian and Corinthian churches were more concerned with their rights than with their responsibilities to God and the church. What about you? Is your focus on getting or giving? Do you more frequently demand your rights or fulfill your responsibilities? Remember that Jesus came not "to be served, but to serve" (Matt. 20:28, NASB). If your focus has gradually changed from ministering to the needs of others to looking out for your own rights, you can help get it back where it belongs by memorizing Philippians 2:3–4.

2. We've learned in this chapter that both men and women can (under the right circumstances) proclaim God's truth. Do you regularly look for opportunities to share the truths of Scripture with your friends, your neighbors, your spouse, or your children? To communicate the truths of

the Bible we must first learn them ourselves. That requires constant study. If you aren't regularly studying Scripture, make a commitment to the Lord to begin today.

# 4: God's
## high calling
## for women
### 1 Timothy 2:12–15

**When Paul gathered** together the Ephesian elders at Miletus in Acts 20:17, and then went on to discuss with them the priorities of ministry, he concluded the discussion with a warning section. That section expressed his deepest fears for that congregation. Beginning in verse 29 Paul says,

> For I know this, that after my departure savage wolves will come in among you, not sparing the flock. Also from among yourselves men will rise up, speaking perverse things to draw away the disciples after themselves. Therefore watch, and remember that for three

years I did not cease to warn everyone night and day
with tears. So now, brethren, I commend you to God
and to the word of His grace, which is able to build you
up and give you an inheritance among all those who
are sanctified. (vv. 29–32)

Paul expressed his great fear that false teachers
would arise within the church as well as come in from
the outside. The church at Ephesus had great and
marvelous beginnings. It was born out of a great revival. It was born out of paganism with a clarity of
purpose and intent that is unsurpassed in the book of
Acts. Yet Paul knew inevitably that no matter how
good the beginning, no matter how effective his own
three-year ministry in that city, it was inevitable that
the enemy would begin to attack that church by bringing in false teachers and unholy leaders to weaken its
effectiveness for God. To be sure, Paul's worst fears
did come to pass. By the time he had finished his first
imprisonment in Rome, he met Timothy in Ephesus
and found that indeed that church of his heart—that
church that had taken so many years of his rather brief
ministry, that church that he loved so deeply, and for
which he no doubt prayed regularly—had fallen prey
to false teachers and those who advocated a godless
living pattern.

So when he and Timothy met there, Paul put out of the church two of the most prominent leaders named in 1 Timothy 1:20—Hymenaeus and Alexander. They were, "delivered unto Satan" (KJV). indicating that Paul himself dealt with them. Then he had to move on west to Greece, leaving Timothy in Ephesus to set the rest of the things right. You'll notice in 3:15 a key to the whole epistle. Paul says, "I write so that you may know how you ought to conduct yourselves in the house of God, which is the church of the living God, the pillar and ground of the truth." In other words, "I'm writing this so you will know how to behave in the church and you can do what you need to do and pass on to the people what they need to hear."

The primary problem in the church at Ephesus was false leadership. Beginning in chapter 3 and running all the way to the end of the epistle, there is a preoccupation with those false leaders. Some chapters are more devoted to this than others, but the theme woven through 1 Timothy 3–6 mainly concerns false leaders. The book then is a polemic against the false leaders who had arisen within the church at Ephesus.

Those false leaders brought to the church a lot of baggage with them. Their ungodliness manifested itself in many ways, including the matter of a woman's role in the church. It is apparent that in Ephesus there were certain women who were desirous of taking the place of official teacher and usurping the leadership authority from the men.

It may well be, though we don't know for certain, that some of those false teachers themselves would not only have advocated a nonbiblical role of women, but were women themselves. That's why Paul in chapter 3 gives the qualifications for an elder as distinctively male qualifications, such as a one-woman man and a man who knows how to manage his own household. So Paul must deal specifically with the role of women in the church before he addresses the false leaders themselves in chapter 3. From verses 9–15, Paul gives us six elements of this very important instruction.

You'll remember that the first thing Paul speaks about is the women's appearance—what external appearance are they to have in church? Verse 9 says women are to cover themselves in a proper adorning. In other words, they are to appear in a way that expresses love for God, reverence for His holiness, and an attitude of worship. The latter part of the verse indicates that they are not to occupy themselves with outward fashion. They are not to flaunt their wealth. He refers to the "plaiting" (or layering) of the hair with gold and pearls, a common cultural custom of that day in which women were so fully clad from neck to the ground that they would flaunt their wealth by their hairstyle. They would weave gold and pearls and place tortoiseshell combs into their hair.

What Paul is saying here is that this practice should not happen in the church. A tendency of women to be occupied with their adornment is only a manifestation of the carnality of their hearts—dressing to flaunt wealth, to attract lust and sexual desire, and to express a spirit of insubordination to one's husband. These are forbidden for a woman who appears to worship God.

Second, as we studied previously, Paul discussed the women's attitude. In the middle of verse 9, we learned that their attitude was to be that of godly fear and self-control. "Godly fear" comes from a root word meaning they have a sense of shame. In other words, women should be ashamed of causing anyone to be distracted from the worship and glory of God. They must have a proper sense of shame that results in modesty. "Self-control" refers to being able to control your passion and desire. Women are to present themselves then in modesty and humbleness of heart, demonstrating total control over their passion and appearing in such a way that draws attention to their godliness and virtue.

Third, in verse 10 we discussed the women's

testimony. If they make a profession of godliness, they should support that with good works. So their deeds should demonstrate that profession of godliness they bear.

That brings us, fourth, to the women's role in verses 11 and 12. This is really the heart of what we're looking at now—their function in the church. The first thing we noted in verse 11 is that the apostle said, "Let a woman learn." We realize that from Jewish and pagan cultures, women were put on a second-class level and their status perhaps was on the level of a slave, in some cases even on the level of animals. There was little concern in the minds of the Jews of that day whether women learned anything or not, since they were really not a part of the educated populous. That segment was to be the men, and the men were responsible for passing on truth. It was immaterial to them whether the women showed up at the synagogue or whether they came to the feasts and festivals.

A similar attitude toward women's education was true in Greek culture. So in contradistinction to all that, Paul said, "Let a woman learn," affirming for us the equality of spiritual privilege, spiritual rights, blessings, and promises for men and women. And as Galatians 3:28 says, In Christ "there is neither male nor female." But in terms of role, Paul qualifies their learning by saying this, "In silence with all subjection" (KJV), and that defines for us the woman's role.

In this chapter, we pick up in verse 12 in our study of a woman's role regarding teaching in the church.

## They Are Not to Teach (v. 12a)

*"I do not permit a woman to teach."*

"Permit" means to allow someone to do what he or she wants. By his word choice, Paul implied that some women at Ephesus had the desire to lead the church. There have always been women who seek leadership roles. Genesis 3:15–16 suggests that part of the result of the Fall was that the woman would desire to control the man, and the man would have to rule over her. The Hebrew word translated "desire" in Genesis 3:16 is used only one other time in the Pentateuch (the first five books of the Old Testament), where it speaks of the desire of sin to control Cain (Gen. 4:7). We can conclude from that usage that Genesis 3:16 is saying women desire to take the control from men.

There are women in the church who are not content with their God-given role. They seek a place of prominence by exercising authority over men. Paul forbade women from taking the authoritative pastor-teacher role in the church. No woman is presented in such an office in the New Testament.

### They Are Not to Have Authority (v. 12b)

*"Or to have authority over a man,
but to be in silence."*

"Have authority" (*authentein*) is used only here in the New Testament. A study of that verb by George Knight concluded that the common meaning of *authentein* in extra-biblical literature is "to have authority over" ("*Authenteō* in Reference to Women in 1 Timothy 2:12," *New Testament Studies*, vol. 30 [1984]: 143–57). He discovered no negative connotation such as "abusing authority."

But what does this *not* mean? First, it indicates that women are not to take abusive authority. Some people have reinterpreted *authentein* in 1 Timothy 2:12 to mean "abusive authority." They believe it is acceptable for women to teach and exercise authority over men as long as their authority does not become abusive. However, there is no justification for this addition to the text. If Paul were speaking of abusive authority, he would not have limited his warning to women.

Teaching and having authority contrast with silence and subjection. Women in the church are not to be in a position where men are subordinate to them.

A second misconception some have taken from this verse is that women are not permitted to pray. However, the phrase "be in silence" in verse 12 is not intended to prohibit women from praying. It teaches that just as women are not to function in the office of teacher or leader in the church, so they are not to lead in the public prayer time of the church.

In addition, this verse does not indicate that women are never to teach. Under some circumstances a woman, along with her husband, could instruct another man. For example, Priscilla and Aquila instructed Apollos (Acts 18:26). However, such instruction would not take place in the public worship service of the church.

Fourth, this verse does not teach that women do not have spiritual gifts. Women can have the same spiritual gifts men have, including the gifts of teaching and leadership. The Lord gives women ample opportunity to use those gifts in a setting that doesn't violate His designed role for them. Women can use those gifts in situations apart from the worship service of the church. Being limited to her God-ordained role in the church and not being permitted to usurp the role of a man in no way wrongs a woman. There is plenty of opportunity for women to exercise their gifts in a manner consistent with God's design.

Fifth, this verse does not teach that women cannot serve as missionaries. I thank God for the many faithful women who serve on the mission field. However, I don't believe women on the mission field have the right to violate their God-ordained role. Paul himself was a missionary. If there was ever a need for leadership on the mission field, it was in his day. Paul could have compromised by using women in leadership roles, but he didn't. When there is a shortage of men on a mission field, the answer is not to violate biblical principles but to pray for the Lord of the harvest to send forth more workers (Matt. 9:38).

Elisabeth Elliot, after the murder of her husband, Jim, and several other missionaries in Ecuador, was the only missionary left who could speak the language of the Auca Indians. She taught one of the Auca men the sermon each week, and he then preached it to the church. We find in her story an excellent example of godly female leadership within the biblical context of allowing men to lead within the gatherings of the church.

Sixth, this verse does not teach that women are inferior to men; they simply have a different role. Many people believe that the only place of power and influence is in a leadership role. They believe it is more fulfilling to lead than to follow. But people in non-leadership roles can be significantly influential as well.

The role of subordination and subjection often brings the greatest peace, happiness, and contentment. The idea that the greatest experience in life is to be on top of the pile and control everything is an illusion. I advise any woman who desires to be a leader in the church to stay under the loving care and protection of her husband and the current church leaders. It's a happier place to be; the burden is significantly lighter.

Subjection is not a punishment; it is a privilege.

## THE DESIGN OF WOMEN (vv. 13–14)

Verses 13–14 make the transition to an additional concept vital to our study—the design of women. We find here that Paul's teachings are based on God's design in creation and were confirmed by the work of the evil one.

## Established by the Creation (v. 13)

*"For Adam was first formed, then Eve."*

God ordained woman's subordinate role in His order of creation. He created Adam first, then Eve. In 1 Corinthians 11:8–9 Paul writes, "The man is not from woman, but the woman from man. Nor was man created for the woman, but woman for the man." She was made to be his helper (Gen. 2:18). She was to follow his lead, live on his provisions, and find safety in his strength and protection through his courage. The tendency to follow was built into Eve, but with the Fall came conflict.

The subordinate role of women is not a cultural issue. It cannot be explained as mere bias on Paul's part, because it is based on the order of creation. Adam was first formed, then Eve.

Nor was Paul's teaching prompted by some cultural situation at Ephesus and therefore not applicable today, as some argue. He not only appeals here to the creation account in Genesis 2, but also taught this same truth to the Corinthians (1 Cor. 11:8–9).

## Confirmed by the Fall (v. 14)

*"Adam was not deceived, but the woman
being deceived, fell into transgression."*

Genesis 3:1–7 (NASB) chronicles the tragic account of what happened in the Garden of Eden when Eve usurped the headship role:

Now the serpent was more crafty than any beast of the field which the Lord God had made. And he said to the woman, "Indeed, has God said, 'You shall not eat from any tree of the garden'?" The woman said to the serpent, "From the fruit of the trees of the garden we may eat; but from the fruit of the tree which is in the middle of the garden, God has said, 'You shall not eat from it or touch it, or you will die.'" The serpent said to the woman, "You surely shall not die! For God knows that in the day you eat from it your eyes will be opened, and you will be like God, knowing good and evil." When the woman saw that the tree was good for food, and that it was a delight to the eyes, and that the tree was desirable to make one wise, she took from its fruit and ate; and she gave also to her husband with her, and he ate. Then the eyes of both of them were opened, and they knew that they were naked; and they sewed fig leaves together and made themselves loin coverings.

The whole human race thus fell into depravity and judgment. Eve was not suited by nature to assume the position of ultimate responsibility. When she stepped out from under the protection and leadership of Adam, she was highly vulnerable and fell. And, of course, when Adam violated his leadership role and followed Eve (though it was not he who was deceived), the perversion of God's order was complete. The Fall resulted, then, not simply from disobedience to God's command, but from violating God's appointed roles for the sexes.

That is not to say that Adam was less culpable than Eve, or that she was more defective. Although he was not deceived by Satan, as was Eve, Adam still chose to disobey God. As the head of their relationship, he bore ultimate responsibility. That is why the New Testament relates the Fall to Adam's sin, not Eve's (Rom. 5:12–21; 1 Cor. 15:21–22). Headship by the man, then, was part of God's design from the beginning, and he bears the responsibility for its success or failure. The tragic experience of the Garden encounter with the serpent confirmed the wisdom of that design.

When we think about the Fall, we usually think of

it in connection with Adam. Romans 5:12–21 speaks repeatedly of the one man (Adam) who brought sin and death into the world. Adam bears responsibility for the Fall, since he is the head of the human race. But we have to keep in mind that he didn't fall first— Eve did. When Eve got out from under the protection of Adam's leadership and attempted to deal independently with the enemy, she was deceived. That reinforces the truth that God designed women with the need for a leader.

Eve showed by her deception that she was unable to lead effectively. She met her match in Satan. The Greek word translated "deceived" (*exapataō*) in verse 14 is a strong term. It is stronger than the common Greek word for "deceived" (*apataō*). It refers to being thoroughly deceived. And so we conclude that when a woman leaves the shelter of her protector she has a certain amount of vulnerability.

The Fall was the result not only of disobeying God's command but also of violating the divinely appointed role of the sexes. Eve acted independently and assumed the role of leadership. Adam violated his role by abdicating his leadership position and following Eve's lead. Nevertheless, it is important to note that women are not more defective than men. And just as women need men, so men need women. We're all vulnerable in different ways.

We affirm the leadership of men because it is established by the creation and confirmed by the Fall. And no daughter of Eve should follow her path and enter into the forbidden territory of leadership that was intended for men.

## THE CONTRIBUTION OF WOMEN (v. 15)

*"Nevertheless she will be saved in childbearing
if they continue in faith, love, and holiness,
with self-control."*

In verse 14 we read of women being in sin. In contrast, verse 15 speaks of women being saved through childbearing. What is Paul saying? All women are saved through childbearing. But saved in what way? What kind of a general statement is this?

The salvation spoken of is not salvation from sin. And it cannot refer to Eve since the future tense is used—"she will be saved." Furthermore, the use of the plural pronoun "they" indicates that more than one woman is in view. It clearly indicates that *all* women are in view.

## Women's Salvation Defined

The Greek word translated "saved" (*sōzō*) can refer to being saved from things other than sin. The word can also mean "to rescue," "to preserve safe and unharmed," "to heal," "to set free," or "to deliver from." It appears a number of times in the New Testament without reference to spiritual salvation (Matt. 8:25; 9:21–22; 10:22; 24:22; 27:40, 42, 49; 2 Tim. 4:18). Paul obviously does not intend to teach that women are eternally saved from the wages of sin through the bearing of children. That would contradict the New Testament's teaching that salvation is by grace through faith alone (Rom. 3:19–20). The future tense and the use of the plural pronoun "they" indicate he was not even referring to Eve. The plural and the absence of any connection to the context also show that Paul was not referring to Mary, the mother of Jesus, as some suggest.

This verse is saying that through childbearing all women are delivered from the stigma of a woman's originating the Fall. A woman led the human race into sin, yet women benefit mankind by replenishing the race. They also have the opportunity to lead the race to godliness through their influence on children.

Women's Significance Delineated

A mother's godliness and virtue can have a profound impact on the life of her children. The rearing of children gives a woman dignity. Her great contribution comes in motherhood. However, she must continue in faith, love, and holiness. Only a godly mother can rear godly children.

Paul teaches here that although a woman precipitated the Fall and women bear that responsibility, yet they may be preserved from that stigma through childbearing. The rescue, the delivery, the freeing of women from the stigma of having led the race into sin happens when they bring up a righteous seed. What a perfect counter to Eve's being deceived! Women are far from being second-class citizens because they have the primary responsibility for rearing godly children. Mothers spend far more time with their children than do their fathers, and thus have the greater influence. Fathers cannot know the intimate relationship with their children that their mother establishes from pregnancy, birth, infancy, and early childhood. Paul's point is that while a woman may have led the race into sin, women have the privilege of leading the race out of sin to godliness.

Obviously, God doesn't want all women to be mothers. Some of them He doesn't even want to be married, since according to 1 Corinthians 7 some have the gift of singleness. Others He allows to be barren for His own purposes. But as a general rule, motherhood is the greatest contribution a woman can make to the human race. The pain of childbearing was woman's punishment for sin, but bearing and rearing children delivers woman from the stigma of that sin.

For women to reverse the blight that has befallen them in the Fall and fulfill their calling they need to bring up a godly seed. To do that, they must continue in faith and love, where their salvation really rests. And they must continue "in holiness, with self-control" (the same word translated "propriety" in verse 9). It is the very appearance, demeanor, and behavior demanded of believing women in the church that becomes their deliverance from any inferior status, as they live godly and rear godly children.

In this passage we see how God has perfectly balanced the roles of the sexes. Men are to be the leaders in the church and the family. Women are kept from any accusation of inferiority through the godly influence they have in the lives of their precious children. For the church to depart from this divine order is to perpetuate the disaster of the Fall.

Paul, under the inspiration of the Holy Spirit, says women are to accept their God-given role. They must not seek the leadership role in the church. Primarily they are to rear godly children. How tragic that so many women feel their lives are unfulfilled because they can't function in the same roles as men. Yet God has given them the unique privilege of rearing a godly generation of children—and of having an intimate relationship with them that no father can know.

Susanna Wesley has gone down in history as one of the greatest Christian mothers. She was the wife of a pastor and the mother of nineteen children. Only about half of those children survived infancy. Two of her sons were John and Charles Wesley, who helped bring revival to England while France was bathed in bloody revolution. Susanna spent one hour each day alone with God in her room, praying for each of her children.

G. Campbell Morgan, the great preacher, said, "My dedication to the preaching of the Word was maternal. Mother never told it to the baby or the boy, but waited. When but eight years old I preached to my little sister and to her dolls arrayed in orderly form before me, my sermons were Bible stories which I had first heard from my mother."

And G. Campbell Morgan, by the way, had four sons, all four of whom became preachers. And on one occasion when Morgan was explaining why all the preachers in his family, someone asked him, "Who is the greatest preacher in your family?"

He replied without hesitation, "My mother."

Charles Spurgeon's father once told an American minister how, when he had often been taken away from home trying to build up congregations, there came a conviction that he was neglecting the religious training of his own children. So he decided that he would preach less. On returning home he opened the door and was surprised to find none of the children around the hall. Ascending the stairs he heard his wife's voice and knew that she was engaged in prayer. One by one she named the children. When she had finished her petition and instruction, the elder Spurgeon said, "I can go on with my work, the children are well cared for."

Now *that* is the role of a godly woman in the church. May God grant us such godly women.

# Review

1. What was one of the reasons Paul wrote 1 Timothy?

2. What was one of the teachings that the false leaders were advocating?

3. The conflict of the sexes was one of the results of _____ .

4. True or false: No woman is ever seen in the role of pastor-teacher in the New Testament.

5. True or false: The Greek word *authentein* is used frequently in the New Testament to refer to abusive authority.

6. What restrictions are placed on a woman's use of her spiritual gifts?

7. What should be done on the mission field when there is a shortage of men for leadership?

8. True or false: Women are not to function in leadership roles because they are inferior to men.

9. Subjection is not a _____; it's a _____ .

10. Why can't Paul's teaching on the subordination of women be dismissed as a cultural bias?

11. In what sense is a woman saved in childbearing?

12. Why can't 1 Timothy 2:15 refer to Eve or Mary? To whom does it refer?

13. True or false: God wants all women to be mothers.

# Reflect

1. Christians today tend to compromise biblical teaching and standards. Under pressure from the feminist movement, some Christians have reinterpreted the Bible's teaching on the role of women. Others have reinterpreted the first few chapters of Genesis in a futile attempt to harmonize the account of creation with the pseudo-science of evolution. Some insist that the Bible does not teach all the principles necessary to address life's problems. The faith "once for all delivered to the saints" (Jude 3, NASB) has too often become like a weather vane—shifting with each passing wind of change. What is the ultimate source of authority in your life? When faced with a conflict between biblical teaching and a contemporary idea, what do you do? Do you reinterpret the Bible or reject the idea? Are you

willing to take a stand for God's Word? Study
Psalm 19:7–11 to see how God describes His
Word, and determine to uphold it.

2. Husbands, how well are you performing your
   role as your wife's protector? Do you protect her
   from physical and emotional harm, or do you
   physically or emotionally abuse her—or let your
   children do so? Do you do everything in your
   power to protect her holiness and purity, or do
   you allow her to be exposed to compromising
   situations? Do you lead by being a sacrificial
   servant or a despotic dictator? Do you make
   your wife's submission to you a heavy burden
   for her to bear? Examine the quality of your love
   for your wife by comparing it with the way
   Christ loves the church. You might wish to begin by meditating on Ephesians 5:25–29.

# Scripture Index